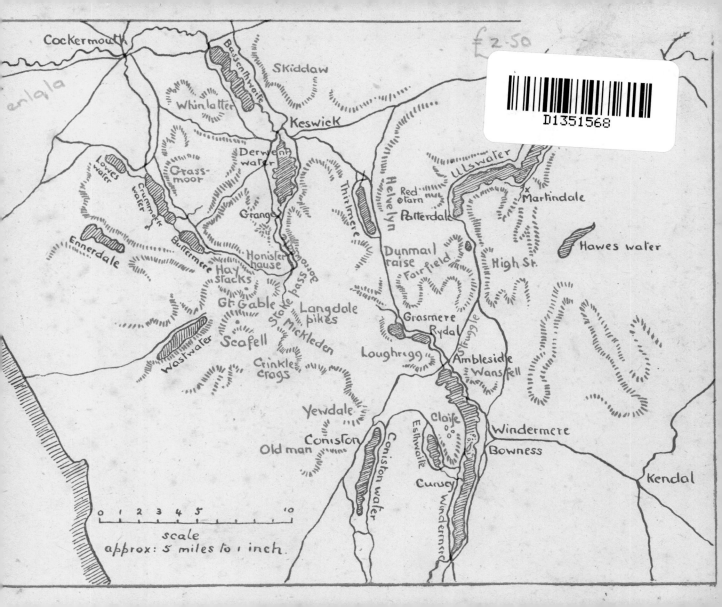

The Lure of Lakeland

Buttermere and Crummock Water
from Birkness Gill

The Lure of Lakeland

by

E. D. TINNE

ILLUSTRATED BY
THE AUTHOR

FREDERICK WARNE & CO. LTD.
LONDON & NEW YORK

THE CALL OF THE NORTH

I must go back. The haunting Northland calls.
The lake, the blue-grey lake at early dawn
When sunbeams catch the top of new-born waves
And cast long shadows on the dewy field
And smile on Mary Rose. And on the fells
The curlews wake and scream and scream again
And new-born lambs join in with plaintive cry.

I know that on the fells, like scattered jewels
Lie the three tarns that are so beautiful,
The one so blue with panoramic view,
And near, but almost hidden by the trees,
The next, the best, all black and shadow-filled.

And there are many becks among the fells,
Joyful, excited ones with waterfalls
And clear green pools that they have worn away,
Cool and inviting on a summer's day,
Like the cool grass where I would love to rest
Gazing below to where the valley lies.

A. G. N. S.

The Lure of Lakeland

What is it about lakes, especially when you find them among mountains? What is it about mountains themselves? Their beauty in the spring with their tops still sprinkled with snow, their sentimental but still lovely colouring in summer, their flaming glory in the autumn, and their hard, bleak grandeur of few colours in the winter. There are the varied skies above them reflected in the lakes, the becks that fall down their steep sides and the rivers that flow through their valleys.

And there's much, oh, much more to it than that. There are birds and trees, flowers and ferns. Huge buzzards soar over the highest crags, or come lower to mew and perch when their young first leave the nest. Ravens live among the mountain-tops and fly past like black shadows, croaking, when they are disturbed. Many sorts of duck visit the lakes; gulls, heron, and kingfishers are permanent residents, waders frequent their shores. The curlew belongs especially to mountain country, and the cry of the first one in March is as welcome as the note of the newly arrived cuckoo in April.

At one time there were more trees in the Lake District than there are now. Huge forests of oak and sycamore have been cut down. Some years ago larches were imported and planted. At first they were very unpopular, but now they are half the charm of Lakeland, adding colour to the fells and making lovely silhouettes against the mountain background.

There are three main entrances to the Lake District if you go by train, Windermere and Coniston from the south, Cockermouth from the north.

If you arrive by Windermere you get the first glimpse of mountains soon after passing through Kendal. It is well worth while to stop there and explore, if you can curb your impatience to be among the hills. The river Kent flows through the town, coming down from the heights above Kentmere.

I should think it was once much deeper than it is now, and navigable right up to Kendal, as there are warehouses along the river bank with steps down the wall, to which boats must have been tied in days gone by. The

Yewdale and Coniston Water

Plate I

town is full of small back-streets and hidden yards, and was built in this intricate way to make it easier of defence in the days of the border raids.

Just before reaching Windermere station you can see the lake on your left, Belle Isle, the southern reach and the tree-covered fells that rise from the western shore.

Some people prefer to arrive at Coniston, where the great mass of Old Man dominates the village and the ancient mine workings all up his steep face give him a somewhat sinister appearance.

Although our own introduction to Lakeland was by Windermere, later experience made us choose Cockermouth to be the ideal starting-place.

The country all around is flat, but, facing south, you see the dim shapes of big mountains filling the horizon; they get bigger and more distinct as you approach, till by the time you are passing Crummock Water they are rising up all round you in truly magnificent size and grandeur.

One grows up in the belief that it is always raining in the Lake District. It certainly rains a good deal. The weather also specialises in sudden and unpredictable changes and even the local inhabitants do not seem to be much good at prophecy.

We were once setting out on a picnic and stopped an old shepherd to ask him if it was going to be fine.

"Aye," he replied, "it'll be fine between the showers."

But if it does rain a lot it does it in a more interesting way than elsewhere. The days between the spells of rain are often so fine, with clear air and sky and bright sun. Then all the fells are streaming with water and the full becks make white streaks down the mountain-sides. It's jolly to sleep in a room with a view of the mountains and to wake up after a cold, wild night following a day of heavy rain, to see the tops all white with snow.

In spring, not the day in March when the spring starts officially, but the real spring in May, I have seen snow lying beneath a blue sky and forming a background to apple-blossom and blackthorn.

One May morning a glorious sunrise had lit up all the snow-covered mountains. We set out early to walk up Wansfel. There was a strong south wind that fairly lifted us up and along. We found a sheltered place behind

E D Tinne

Plate II   Snow on High Street in May

a rock and lunched in comparative warmth. Afterwards we went on. Soon we reached the snow-line and there found drifts three and four feet deep. The sky was deep blue with little white clouds. Snow was thick on High Street and behind the Kirkstone Pass the mountain-tops were all pure white.

We went on through the gate on the top of Wansfell and down the wild and unknown side against a tearing, bitter, icy wind. But what a view! The sea, from Barrow to Grange and then the hills over Kendal, and beyond, the Pennines, all snow-covered.

Between the drifts in the foreground the snow had melted and the grass was a dark and vivid green, starred all over with celandine and wild violets. We turned south and found a green valley full of sheep and lambs. All around were rocks and short, crisp heather. A red grouse rose just in front of us and sailed down the fell. Then we crossed a beck very full of snow water, deep brown and full of bubbles, running over and under the grass and plunging into deep, dark pools. We reached the bridge in Robin Lane and went on down the beck.

Winter with its snow and icy wind was left behind, we stepped down into the deep gorge of the beck and walked straight into spring; soft green grass, oak leaves opening deep gold, birch leaves yellow-green, and rowan greenest of all. Down the flat rock cliff on the opposite side from us water was streaming in long, lacy falls, seen through the green veil of newly opened leaves.

From High Skelghyl on to Ambleside the road was edged with bird cherries in full flower and bluebells were opening in the woods.

That is spring in Westmorland, snow and flowers, icy wind and sun, cloudy skies and clear; while lambs are being born, trees coming into leaf, bracken fronds uncurling, and the walls cast darker shadows as the days get longer.

No one visits Lakeland without knowing and loving the Langdale Pikes; they are a landmark to be hailed with friendly familiarity from all around.

Langdale itself is a lovely valley, rather mysterious and uncanny, we always felt, with the old gunpowder works at its entrance and the quiet remoteness of its far end. The old coach-road runs below the present road. On one occasion we determined to go by it and think, meanwhile, of bygone days, of coaches and four-in-hands. But we found it all stones. It was more like the bed of a beck than a road, and all our attention was taken up with the difficulty of getting our bicycles along.

When you reach the end of Langdale you feel that you have come to the end indeed; but a stony road goes on and leads you either up Oxendale and so to Bow Fell, or to the right through Mickleden. Then at the end of that valley, you have a choice again; a long climb to the left up to Esk Hause or right, to Stake Pass leading over into Borrowdale.

It was on the way up Harrison Stickle, one of the Langdale Pikes, that I first found mountain parsley, the fern that grows in the crevices of nearly every rock above a certain altitude. The mountain moss is, of course, sphagnum, famous for its use as a surgical dressing. It is very soft and always full of water and turns the most lovely colours ranging from palest whitey-yellow, through russet and green to deep orange and crimson.

I was once walking over a big expanse of sphagnum beside a beck. I saw a spotted orchis and then another, growing amongst groups of rushes and buttercups. A little farther on I noticed more and then came into a regular garden of them. They were scattered down the fell side as though broadcast by some giant hand, some deep crimson, others mauve and some white, all beautifully spotted and marked as if they had been drawn upon with a fine pen.

There is a good view of the Langdale Pikes from Wansfell, that mountain of such easy access from Ambleside.

Here is a piece of grassy, bracken-covered fell that we christened the "Playground". There are big outcrops of rock all about it that give splendid climbing practice and some of them have small cliffs that can be tackled with a rope. Higher up you come to the first of Wansfell's many walls. These have to be negotiated with care. Like all the walls in Lakeland they are dry-stone, that is to say, built without mortar, and it is an easy and disgraceful thing to bring any of the stones down as you climb over.

Walls form a conspicuous part of the landscape in the Lake District. Some go straight up and over a mountain in one long, leaping line, taking any gradient in their stride: others wander about, have curves and corners and make lovely patterns on the fells.

Bow Fell and Langdale Pikes
from the top of Loughrigg

E D Tinne

Plate III

It is difficult to say which is one's favourite lake, one loves each for something different.

Rydal Water is happy and friendly, good to walk around, good to bathe in and boat on, and lovely for skating nearly every winter. Being close under the north side of Loughrigg it gets little sun in winter and freezes early. Cold winds blow upon it from the north, coming by way of Dunmail Raise and Grasmere. Even on the hottest day in summer the water is cold. It is often a more spartan matter to bathe there than in Windermere.

If you look north from Rydal Water, at the steep face of Nab Scar, you will be almost sure to see buzzards perched on a rock against the sky or wheeling in slow circles, high up. Beyond and behind Nab Scar, out of sight of the lake or the road, are Lord Crag and Heron Pike. It is on one of these that the buzzards usually nest.

One day I was walking through Rydal Park when I heard a mewing cry. There were three buzzards high above me. Two were chasing the third, which seemed to be doing its best to get away. One caught up with it, they came to grips and fell rapidly till they were nearly tree-top height, a struggling

Rydal Water

Plate IV

mass of flapping wings and claws. Then they fell apart, a few feathers floated down and the chase continued across Rydal Water and away over Loughrigg beyond. The remaining buzzard perched on the dead branch of an oak till the others were out of sight, then it rose and flew slowly back over Nab Scar.

During our very first summer at Ambleside we decided that we could not possibly live so near a lake and not possess a boat. So we bought one and no sum of money was ever better spent. Our boat was worth her weight in gold. Seeking something really safe for the children I discussed the matter with a local boat-builder. I suggested a dinghy, good and broad in the beam and about eight feet long.

"Aye," Mr. Woods replied, "but I should have a ten-foot, lady, and even then she'll be rather tŭb."

And so a ten-foot dinghy was ordered. She was built in Ipswich, care being taken to use no elm in her construction as it rots at once in the water of Windermere.

"Spruce, lady, or mahogany," Mr. Woods said, "but don't have no ellum; ellum's no good here."

One April day, she came, from Ipswich to Windermere by train, from Windermere to Waterhead by lorry, and was launched with due ceremony. She was given the name of "Dabchick", for she was indeed rather tŭb, and the Dabchick is a tŭb little bird.

She is entered on the first page of the log-book as Rowing Vessel Dabchick, her port Waterhead. Then follow the signatures of the skipper, the able-seaman, the ship's boy, and the mark of the ship's dog. On the next page there is an account of her launching and first trip, with this poem at the page head:

"We christened her at Waterhead
    And bathed her stern in tea
Then pushed her down the shelving beach
    Into the inland sea.
The Skipper, A.B. and the Boy
    Each took an oar in hand
And pulled in all directions
    To reach a distant land."

Plate V   Windermere

The dream dinghy had become a real dinghy, a smart little boat of Canadian spruce and mahogany, resplendent with golden varnish.

"I almost wish we hadn't got her," the A.B. had said when we walked down the lane to the lake before launching. "It was so glorious looking forward to having her."

The regret soon passed when we embarked, with the Skipper on the bow thwart with two oars, and the A.B. and the Boy on the centre thwart with an oar apiece. The style of the rowing was erratic to begin with but soon improved, and the first trip was a success.

For two summers we were satisfied.

And then we grew ambitious, for far horizons called us; we could see down the lake to the islands, indeed we had even rowed as far, but un-explored waters lay beyond. We decided we must have a sail. Something simple and not too big and a mast not too high; it was all to be correct and most exciting, but quite safe.

A boat-builder in Bowness hunted up some "bits" for mast and boom, a beautiful piece of mahogany for a rudder, and a spinnaker sail that had never been used. They were taken back to Waterhead in triumph and all spread on the path by the lake, causing great obstruction to the passers-by. Mr. Woods joined the conference and we crawled about, planning the boom, the yard ("or is it the gaff, lady?"), and the sail. The boom and the gaff ("or is it the yard, lady?") were taken off to be cut the right length and the mast to be fitted forward of the bow thwart. The sail was brought home, and my sewing-machine did valiant work turning it into a standing lug.

Our favourite short cruise was straight across the head of Windermere to the Brathay shore where we found and named "Mallard Bay", "Gull Rocks", "Conversation Cove", "The Bathing Bay", and "Cherry Circle".

A pair of Mallard, of course, gave the name to the first big bay, but later a pair of peewits nested there close to a pair of nesting redshank. The peewit used to fly around screaming and imploring us to go away, while the redshank ran round in nervous little circles on the grass. Gull Rocks and Conversation Cove were always full of talkative gulls; herring gulls, lesser black-backed, black-headed and an occasional kittiwake. A pair of cormorants

Windermere, looking North from
Ling Holme

sometimes came to the big rock in Bathing Bay and sheld duck were seen near there in early spring.

Cherry Circle was a grove of enormous old cherry trees, and cherries must have been the favourite food of the gulls considering the amount of pellets we found on the rocks, composed entirely of cherry stones. Curlew frequented the field between the shore and the woods, but they rarely came very near the water.

The woods themselves are a grand place for flowers. In some parts of the Lake District they are a sea of bluebells in spring, while in others daffodils grow and flower thickly under the trees. Bluebells border the paths and roads, and in some of the valleys daffodils edge the becks. Where trees have been felled foxgloves spring up, and continue blooming there every summer till new trees grow again and shade them, when they will die away and their seeds lie dormant in the soil once more, perhaps for many years, till their next opportunity for growth.

In one wood that we knew, oak had been felled and the first time we went there after the felling it was full of foxgloves. By the next year a growth of broom seedlings was springing up. Two summers later the wood was filled with tall brooms, waving their vivid yellow blossoms in the sun, while blue-bells flowered round the edges. The colour was dazzling.

Our best voyages were southward to the islands and beyond. We could sail to the islands in two hours with a favourable breeze, and they are all fascinating to explore. So is the long reach of the lake south of the ferry.

High Cunsey is a cluster of houses and farms on the west or Lancashire side of the lake. The little Wilfin Beck comes down from Moss Eccles tarn on Claife Heights, runs under a barn and a bridge and across a field into the lake. It is a beautiful and busy little beck, full of fish, bordered with black-berries, the happy home of grey wagtails, farmyard ducks and a dipper who, in winter, no matter how cold the weather is, perches each morning on a favourite stone and sings the sweetest song.

We were picking blackberries by the beck one day in summer when the Boy noticed a dragonfly dart by in pursuit of a wasp. It caught it and settled on a low thornbush. We knelt quietly down on one side and watched. The

View from the old barn,
built over Wilfin Beck,
High Cunsey

Plate VII

"armour-plating" of its face opened into four sections, the top and bottom ones worked up and down, the other two from side to middle. And so it munched and munched until the wasp had slowly disappeared. It took about two minutes before the tips of the wasp's hind legs had disappeared, and then the "armour-plating" closed and the dragonfly resumed its customary inscrutable expression. We left it there, digesting.

There are good, strong, south-west winds at this end of Windermere. They come roaring up from Lakeside and either whip the water into quite big waves or cause a rolling swell that makes you feel the sea cannot really be so very far away. The cormorants give a sea feeling too; they are often seen on the lake or flying up and down, low over the water. Several pairs of sheld duck frequent the bays in the spring and parties of other duck are seen in autumn and winter.

The woods and hedgerows at Cunsey are nearly always full of flowers and a different colour scheme seems to grace each season. In June pink is the fashion, the hedges being festooned with wild roses, while solid ranks of fox-gloves stand beneath. Each rabbit-hole in the banks around the fields seems to

27

have a foxglove sentinel beside it. In August, soft shades of mauve and yellow appear, drifts of scabious making sheets of colour against the pale yellow of the oat-fields. Knapweed and betony share the hedgerows with St. John's wort and hawkbits. Birds and butterflies add to the brilliance of these flowers, linnets twitter along the roadside and goldfinches are everywhere, like little bits of singing sunshine.

The old barn which straddles the beck was built originally for the barrel hoopmakers, who used to soak the withies for the hoops in the running water beneath the floor. Another barn, now converted into a house is even older. It is on the edge of the lake and used to be a boathouse, where the iron ore from the mines at Graythwaite was loaded into a barge to be carried down to Lakeside. There was no road down the western shore of Windermere in olden days.

There is a big headland, called Rawlinson's Nab, a little farther down the lake. Whatever the direction of the wind, one side of it is always sheltered. There is a broad beach of grey pebbles on the southern side, which is the best place for bathing in all Windermere.

Fairfield from Wansfell ("the Playground")
in Spring

Plate VIII

We had picnicked on the northern side one day, having rowed down in "Dabchick"! We were hoping to sail back. We could see there was a good south wind, as the ripples were streaming north past the headland. The big bay before us was calm with occasional little catspaws of wind chasing across it. So we hoisted sail and moved slowly forward, thinking we would soon turn to port and start sailing north. Suddenly a strong westerly gust hit us, "Dabchick" heeled over, jibbed violently, and we found ourselves racing across the lake towards the eastern shore! The Boy went forward with great promptitude and lowered sail. It had been a thrilling and an alarming moment, and we had a long row back.

That was the only time I have seen contradictory winds competing with each other on Windermere. After this episode we treated the lake with more respect.

There are always rather eccentric winds in mountain country, but the worst, iciest, most tearing gale I ever met was on the top of Fairfield. It is a mountain that looms large in one's life at Ambleside. It is a definite barrier to the north; its appearance is supposed to indicate the weather to expect and nearly every morning we looked at Fairfield, especially whenever we wanted to decide about an outing on a doubtful looking day.

The walk up Scandale Fell, round the saucer-like rim of Fairfield and down by Nabscar is a popular one, and it was a walk I always meant to take. But somehow the opportunity never seemed to come along, or if it did I was slow to seize it. Quite often I got as far as High Pike, or the head of Scandale Beck, and I went up Nabscar from Rydal, but I never got the whole way round. At last it seemed that Fairfield had become a challenge that I must accept.

And so on the very maddest day I could have chosen, I went. It was fine with a bright February sun, a north wind, and a sky of grey and white clouds. I set off, got up Scandale Fell, pushing against the wind, and had lunch in the shelter of a rock while I watched a sheepdog collecting sheep from the sky-line to the valley beneath.

The speed with which they can go right up the fell is amazing. They find each sheep and bring it at a steady pace, not too fast, to join the others. Sheep in two's and three's came together and joined other two's and three's, trailing along the fellside like strings of grey pearls, and finally in the valley

Ullswater, looking south
from the path
to Sandwick

Plate IX

bottom, joined the ever-enlarging flock that was being taken along to the head of Scandale.

In the bracken country of the Lake District the sheepdogs are long-legged, and often look as if there were a bit of hound in them. Over to the east of the county smaller black-and-white collies are more usual.

After lunch I went on, over a low and uninteresting expanse of yellow grass and wondered which would be the better way down, across towards Red Screes and back by Snarker Pike, or down Scandale Beck. Fairfield looked dark and uninviting. I decided I would only go that way if I turned west by 2.30. I did, so I went on, meaning to decide finally how far I could go when I got to a certain rock. I reached it and looked back.

What a long way I had come! It was a dull stretch behind me, and I did not want to retrace my steps; the unknown before seemed more attractive than the known behind. Unfortunately I had forgotten to bring a map, one look at which would have decided otherwise.

And so I went on. Up a rocky staircase first, well worn by other climbers' hobnailed boots, and marked at frequent intervals by small cairns. Down the

33

Plate X

St. Martin's Old Church, Martindale,
Ullswater

other side and then—I met it! A thousand-mile-an-hour wind, seemingly direct from the Arctic, coming by way of Ullswater straight up Deepdale and slipping over Fairfield like water over a weir. I have never even tried to stand against such a wind, and certainly not to walk. Indeed, walking was impossible. I had to lie down and then crawled on, clinging to a rock every now and then as I paused to rest.

It was hard to look towards the north at all as it felt as though my eyelids would be torn off, but the view was well worth the effort. I could see Ullswater and the mountains beyond all dark and snow-capped. To the south was visible all the coastline, Kendal estuary, the hills beyond and nearer, all the lakes between; Windermere, Coniston, Esthwaite, Blelham, little Moss Eccles. Later, after staggering on, and up, I found myself looking down on Grisedale Tarn, a dark pool with a snowy rim.

I progressed, when I could stand up, in a series of short runs, always starting off towards the right, and being blown to the left so that I steered a zigzag course. The ground was very rough and frozen hard.

"What if I sprain my ankle now," I thought, and tried to be careful.

35

I hoped for less wind when I turned towards the south, but it was as strong as ever from a north-westerly direction, and came streaming up the fellside. It blew so hard I felt I might be picked up bodily to be whirled away down the Rydal Beck, and deposited at the back door of Rydal Hall!

Up and down, up and down, up and down. At last I came to clumps of frosty brown bracken and some sheep. I was so pleased to see them I could have clasped them round their woolly necks in my relief. Soon I was standing in the road at Rydal waiting for the 4.15 bus. I looked back.

"I've been up there!" I thought, "I've been round, I've done it!"

I had done it, in four and a half hours; it is a twelve-mile walk and the highest point over 2,000 feet. I wonder shall I ever go again on a fine, suitable day?

The lake most famous for peculiar winds is Ullswater.

The most curious effect of wind I ever saw was one day when gusts were coming down the mountain-sides in all directions upon Ullswater. The surface of the water was picked up and a tall column went twisting and

Thirlmere's Islands

Plate XI

whirling down the lake in a halo of spray, while little waves were dancing round its base.

At the head of the lake, where the Goldrill enters it, there is a considerable delta carrying a growth of birches, willows, and reeds. It is a good place for birds: pied fly-catchers, grey wagtails, sedge-warblers, and reed-buntings can be seen, and it is favourite hunting-ground for heron, too.

We were coasting quietly along in "Dabchick" one day (she had been taken over the Kirkstone Pass and put on Ullswater for the holidays), and as we went past an open boathouse we saw a heron inside. Birds seem to notice a moving boat less than a moving person, and we got quite close. He walked along one side of the boathouse, peering into the water, went round the end and down the other side, quite oblivious of our presence. He kept peering intently into the water, then suddenly leant forward, thrust out and down, and caught a fish. Then he saw us, spread his great wings slowly, launched himself unhurriedly upon the air and flew away. We rowed into the boat-house and found the shallow water just full of fish.

There is a good walk along a narrow path on the east side of the lake.

Skiddaw from the valley of the
River Derwent

Plate XII

The fell rises steeply above it and drops away as steeply beneath, and it is easy to imagine the slope going straight on and on into a great depth of water. It leads to Sandwick, a farm in a lovely sheltered valley, and then joins a narrow road that leads to Martindale, a tiny village in a remote valley with a very old church. From here you can go on round the northern end of Ullswater and over Pooley Bridge, which is about five miles south of Penrith.

On one expedition we went up Glenridding to Red Tarn, which lies in the curve of Helvelyn. We reached the foot of Swirrel Edge but did not fancy the ascent, even had a strong wind not been blowing. We lay on our fronts and looked over it right away to the Solway Firth and the hills of Scotland beyond.

In Glenridding we were shown over the lead mines and brought little pieces of ore away with us. The waste from this mine drains into the beck and runs down into the lake like milk. It was curious when we were in "Dabchick" to remember that the galleries of the mine were far below us beneath the floor of the lake.

Thirlmere is a lake that you may pass by, admiring it as you go, but never finding an opportunity to stop there and explore. It is between Grasmere and Keswick, being some seven miles from one and nine from the other. It is well worth seeing in more detail than you can from bus or car on the main road, so aim to leave the bus or stop your car with the determination to make its acquaintance.

Thirlmere is one of the lakes that supplies Manchester with water, and it is because of this, perhaps, that it is different from the others. My own feeling is that it does not look English. I do not know if this is because of the larches and conifers planted so thickly on all the surrounding fells, or if it is the lovely colours they reflect into the water, but I hardly ever go there without being made to think of Italy, or the South of France. Going past the lake on a sunny day you get glimpses of the water between the trees, a true "Mediterranean blue".

Once we went when the colouring was of a different kind. It was winter, or rather the very end of winter, when on fine days there is a hint of spring in the air. Blackbirds were singing and there were catkins on the hazels.

Plate XIII

View across the south end of
Bassenthwaite to Whinlatter

We went by bus to Swathwaite Bridge at the north end of the lake, and walked all round the western shore. We had just reached the dam—the road goes across the top of it—when we heard a musical clamour above us, and looking up saw a big skein of geese flying north. They were in a wide double V, then changed position and went on in a long single one. They were heading straight into a clear blue sky and sunshine, the only cloud in sight being a fluffy belt round the top of Skiddaw.

We crossed the dam, turned south and found ourselves looking into a flat wall of cold mist rising slowly into the sky. The sun shone through it looking like a white moon, and we walked into an icy wind from the southwest. But the colouring was wonderful, a symphony of black and silver with a hint of blue in the grey water and a little sunlight filtering through the mist and touching up the mountains with green and palest gold. Two more skeins of geese passed over, adding the last touch of weird wildness to the scene.

When we came level with the islands we noticed that the lake was covered with long parallel lines of bubbles, all flowing down towards the dam. We counted fifteen between us and the opposite shore, and wondered what

43

Plate XIV

Where the River Derwent enters
Bassenthwaite

strange freak of wind and weather produced this curiosity. If you never knew Thirlmere before it was harnessed by Manchester, and that was a long time ago now, it is possible to love it very much for its present beauty.

Not so with Hawes Water. Our first visit was just after the completion of the great dam astride the valley. We went along the road beside the lake and felt sadder and sorrier with every step we took. On the far side, the walls that had once enclosed the fields belonging to now-drowned farms, ran forlornly down to the lake. And when we reached Mardale, or what remained of Mardale, we found the houses, the hotel, and the church, all heaps of rubble, the streets grass-grown and a few sheep wandering among the ruins. It was all too horrible. We picked up some fragments of coloured tiles from the remains of the church and came away.

I wonder if future generations will ever hear the church bells ringing from deep below the surface of the water of Manchester's second lake!

As you approach Keswick from the south you get a glimpse of Derwentwater below on the left and can see the end of Bassenthwaite in front beyond the town. The river Greta runs close beside the road at the bottom of the hill and joins the river Derwent just north of the lake. The valley between the two lakes is wide and green and can be seen to the best advantage if you take the track beside the river instead of going on either of the roads.

The huge mass of Skiddaw towers on your right, his lofty head invariably wrapped in cloud.

Whinlatter rises above the fells to the left; presently you see a narrow bridge, and crossing it, come to higher ground leading up to the road that skirts Skiddaw as it travels north.

Bassenthwaite lies at your feet. It is a lovely lake that seems to be little visited; the fells on its western side are tree-covered. The Derwent enters the lake between reed-beds and flat, marshy islets, and the water takes on the most lovely colours, deep blue, sea-green, purple, and even yellow.

Keswick is known as the best centre in the Lake District from which to make expeditions. It is certainly on the threshold of most exciting country

Looking across Derwentwater
from Cat Bells

Plate XV

and exploration can be made all around, by road, by water, or by mountain pass. Derwentwater was the only lake, I believe, where a launch continued to run all through the war, going down to Lodore after calling at the western shore.

We first got to know the country round Keswick in winter, or what is usually winter, but was trying its best to be a very early spring. The hazels were hung with catkins and many more little crimson tufts than usual, which shone like rubies when the light caught them. Bluebell leaves were an inch high in the woods, blackbirds and thrushes were singing, ringdoves were cooing, and the curlew had arrived a full month earlier than usual. For it was February and a month of such strange variety of weather that it made our expeditions even more interesting than usual.

The day we explored Derwentwater was warm and springlike. To begin with, the sky was full of heavy grey clouds, the sun shining through in long, pale shafts; higher still, the cloud edges were vivid white against a very blue sky. As we went down the lake we saw a great northern diver, swimming close inshore, also a small party of whooper swans.

We crossed the river at Grange, which is the gateway of Borrowdale, and then turned to go up the western shore of the lake and so back to Keswick. As we reached the highest part of the road, there was a short shower, and, as the sky cleared, a rainbow spanned the air right to our feet. Then we saw that all the tops were snow-covered.

If instead of crossing over the bridge at Grange you go through the gateway of Borrowdale and then on, new country opens out before you, all ringed around with grand, high mountains. It is always fascinating to find places "linking up". You can know a valley well, climb the mountains that surround it, and become familiar with all its rocks and becks. Then one day you will be far away exploring another valley; you stop to take a look at the map, trace the direction that you are taking, see a pass and, suddenly, there is the familiar valley just waiting for you, apparently, on the other side of the mountains.

This happened to us in Borrowdale. We knew Langdale well and had explored up Mickleden and gone as far as Stake Pass but never over it. Then

49

Plate XVI

Castle Crag from
Grange in Borrowdale

we made the acquaintance of Borrowdale, and one day found a "footpath to Stake Pass", a link with our familiar valley from another that had, until then, seemed so very far away.

Through Rossthwaite and on to Seatoller is one of the bus routes, but having reached this point it then stops in a very final manner, having gone into the mountains till, it seems, they completely bar the way. And so you leave it and start to walk or climb up the long, steep hill to Honister Hause, over that impressive pass and so on down to Buttermere. After the descent we were greeted by four whooper swans on the lake, and later saw a pair of goldeneye, the drake vivid black-and-white, his wife scarcely visible against the water.

Buttermere lies in the shadow of Red Pike, High Stile, High Crag, and the Haystacks. There is a good track over Scarth Gap beside the Haystacks, which takes you by an easy path, though a long one, to the head of Ennerdale Water. But you need a fine day and sun, I think, to go that way.

We felt the Haystacks had a frowning, almost a threatening look, in their great height, their darkness, and their frequent cloak of cloud.

They have that "feeling" that seems so often associated with mountains containing old mine workings, something remote and mysterious, slightly uncanny.

Crummock Water is a most beautiful lake; looking across it from Sail Beck, which runs beside part of Buttermere Hause, the view is filled with mountain-tops. The path close beside the western shore is lovely, too; you can walk right round the lake or turn aside at the mouth of the Scale Beck and follow it up to Floutern Tarn.

Grassmoor is the highest mountain near the northern end of Crummock Water, and is a mountain of a curious shape, looking squarely flat-topped when seen from the north of Derwentwater, and a simple "sugar loaf" like a child's drawing of a mountain, when seen from Crummock Water.

The bird life is interesting round Buttermere and Crummock Water. The two lakes are close together, both are surrounded by high mountains, and yet the bird inhabitants are most distinct. We have never seen so many ravens as there were at Buttermere or so many buzzards as we saw round Crummock Water. One is so used to meeting a solitary raven, or at most

Buttermere and the Haystacks

Plate XVII

two, on the tops, that it was extraordinary to see a large flock indulging in aerial acrobatics close to the lake the whole of one windy morning.

Circling, tumbling, soaring, round and round they went and then several left the main flock and flew across the lake towards us. Quite close above us, they continued their antics, wings closed for a moment, a side slip, a twist over, then vigorous flaps to regain height, and all the time croaking and making loud "clacks". There was a strong north-west wind blowing and whether it helped them or not we could not tell. Perhaps it had an exhilarating effect on them; they certainly seemed hilarious and excited.

All round Crummock Water the sound most frequently heard was the mewing of the buzzard. We saw two pairs on the west side and one pair on the east. They were mostly flying low, those on the western shore dipping amongst the trees or circling just above them. On the other side we watched one flying in lovely rhythmic loops all along the steep, rocky face of the fell, appearing and disappearing, as first its light underside and then its darker back showed alternately against the grey and brown of the heather-covered rocks.

Crummock Water and the Haystacks
from Low Banks

Plate XVIII

Of small birds in this valley, chaffinches were the most plentiful, but there were also many yellow-hammers, for flashes of brilliant yellow appeared in the hedges and the plaintive jingle about "no cheese" was heard perpetually, whether the day was fine and sunny, wild and windy, or teeming with rain under a leaden sky.

The skies of the Lake District are extraordinarily varied. In a place where there is so much rain there is, of course, a lot of cloud. The sky is hardly every entirely clear, for even if a day should commence cloudless sooner or later they begin to appear.

Thin, wispy trails of cloud will drift between Hart Crag and Fairfield, travelling in a south-westerly direction, or big cotton-woolly cumulus clouds will poke their heads above the northern horizon and slowly mounting the sky begin their stately journey south, to be joined a little later by others coming up from east and west, and so the sky will gradually fill.

Quite often there are lovely composite skies, huge, tumbled grey and white cumulus against a background of a high mackerel sky, or there will be layers of clouds travelling in opposite directions pushed by contrary winds at different heights. Occasionally we see the rare mammato-cumulus clouds, those queer shapes that hang motionless in the same place nearly all day and look like smooth, rounded pices of marble.

The skies, beautiful by day, excel at dawn and sundown. Often the colour spreads from one horizon to the other and lasts a long time. Frequently the sunsets are so magnificent that people stand outside their houses to watch the wealth of colour spreading across the heavens.

There is one sunset, seen from Buttermere, which is famous for ripening the harvest!

The sunrise is not seen so easily. Often the pageant is over by the time people are astir. But if you wish to see a really lovely dawn, go and spend the night—or half the night—at the foot of Helvelyn; get up before it is light, and be at the top in time to greet the sun. You can only do this in summer, of course, when the weather is warm enough to allow of sleeping out.

In Lakeland, the weather must be ignored, the good taken with the bad, the fine with the wet. The best effects of light and colour are often seen in the worst of weather. If it were always fine and sunny you would never know

E.D.Tinne

Plate XIX   Crummock Water from Sail Beck

how impressive the mountains can be when dark under a stormy sky, or pale and mysterious through a veil of rain. If it were always warm you would never see them under snow or feel the air, iced as it is in the first days of autumn.

Autumn begins early in Lakeland. Bracken is already beginning to be touched with brown in August, by Michaelmas the early mornings are nicely iced, and days of brilliant sun only come in between the days of wind and rain. The swifts have gone, but a few swallows are still to be seen and quite a lot of house-martins. The sky is so full of them some days that one feels there is no need to think of losing them yet. Then suddenly they are gone, and one hasn't even said good-bye.

By the beginning of October the stage is set for the pageant of autumn, and if the weather be kind, there will be a grand performance. Birches go yellow from inside outwards, the leaves near the trunk change colour first, while the outer ones are still green. Horse chestnuts do it the other way round, and hang festoons of yellow, pink, and orange down the outside against a background of deep green leaves. Oaks sprout little patches of gold

Plate XX

Hawes Point, Crummock Water, from
the mouth of Scale Beck

all through, and sycamores acquire a burnished look, as shades of dark bronze and old rose creep over their blue-green leaves before they all turn bright orange. Beeches simply glow with colour, every shade of yellow, gold and orange.

But the wild cherries are the best! Going down Windermere in autumn one sees them flaming out amongst the other trees all through the woods on the western shore, just pure crimson, more brilliant than all the other trees in autumn dress.

We sailed up from Bowness to Waterhead one day in October, our last trip before "Dabchick" was laid up for the winter. I rang up our friend the boat-builder, who said it was a flat calm down by the islands. He had had charge of "Dabchick" ever since we had been at Cunsey in the summer holidays, and we were anxious to get her up to Waterhead again before the winter.

We packed lunch, put on lots of warm clothes, took extra scarves and jerseys and caught a bus. We found the water in Bowness Bay right over the landing-stage and inside the big boatshed. "Dabchick" was fetched for us and brought round to the beach. A southerly wind was springing up and we set sail at once for a small island, the first one towards the north. We landed there and found it a most romantic little place with a steep rock cliff to the north, and a queer "table" of three huge slabs of stone, where we had our lunch. Afterwards we embarked again, and our real voyage began. There was a spanking south wind by this time, and once past the north end of "Long Island" we were struck by the full force of it. "Dabchick" simply lifted along, big waves following us, and every now and then breaking under our stern and running past on each side of us with a long, bubbly "shush-sh-sh-".

We saw a large flock of duck on the water and sailed straight towards them. They rose, flew towards the western shore and settled again. They were goldeneye. Then we turned back on our course and settled down to run to the far north. The lake was like molten lead and the pale sun coming between ragged grey clouds made a silvery polished pathway over the waves. We were only just warm enough, and pretty stiff when we arrived at Waterhead after a sail of one and a half hours that felt almost like a voyage of days!

Grassmoor, Crummock Water

Plate XXI

Autumn ends the seasons as sunsets end the day, each with a promise of what is to follow. After autumn, winter and then spring. After sundown, night and then dawn. But often in this lovely corner of England, dawns which herald most unexpected days. No use the adage "red at night is the shepherd's delight" in the Lake District. In the midst of dark winter weather summer days will suddenly appear, when frosts seem to foretell a spell of fine weather, then the next day will be wet. No ordered rhythm in the pattern of the days, the unexpected always.

What then is the Lure of Lakeland? Is it the beauty of the lakes or the grandeur of the mountains?

Well, why not go and find out for yourself?